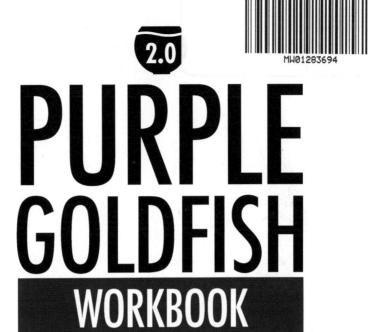

# PURPLE GOLDFISH

## WORKBOOK

**HOW TO IMPLEMENT PURPLE GOLDFISH STRATEGY IN YOUR ORGANIZATION**

Name:

_____

Date:

_____

## WELCOME

Welcome to the *Purple Goldfish Workbook*. We're glad you're here! Using the process in this workbook you'l be able to create differentiation, drive customer loyalty, and create positive word-of-mouth. All by focusing on the little things that make a big difference to your customers.

The *Purple Goldfish Workbook* is a great companion to *Purple Goldfish 2.0*, which highlights examples from hundreds of companies that have successfully created their own Purple Goldfish. We'll start out with an executive summary of *Purple Goldfish 2.0* and then dig into our I.D.E.A. Process.

We look forward to serving as your guide. Let's dive in!

## TABLE OF CONTENTS

## PART ONE: 10 CUSTOMER EXPERIENCE TAKEAWAYS

### #1. What's the Biggest Myth in Marketing?

The biggest myth in marketing is the ideas of meeting expectations. There is no such thing as meeting expectations. You either exceed them or you fall short. In a world where 60-80 percent of customers describe themselves as satisfied or very satisfied before going on to defect to other brands, merely "meeting expectations" is no longer an option.

### #2. Two Paths Diverge in the Corporate Woods

You can't be all things to all people. You only have two choices as a marketer: Create to spec and face being a commodity or set out to exceed expectations and become remark-able. Choose wisely...

### #3. Shareholders vs. Customers?

Business is about creating and keeping customers. Customer experience should be Priority #1 in your marketing. Stop focusing on the "two in the bush" (prospects) and take care of the one in your hand (customers).

### #4. Value is the New Black

Don't compete on price. Cater to the seventy percent that buy based on value. Price is only relative to the value received.

### #5. Corollary to the Pareto Principle

Traditional marketing is flawed. Eighty percent of your efforts will net twenty percent of your results. Focus on existing customers instead of the funnel by finding little extras that are tangible, valuable and talk-able.

## #6. Growth is Determined by Five Factors

The growth of your product or service is similar to that of a goldfish. Growth is determined by five factors:

1.    Size of the bowl = Market

2.    Number of other goldfish in the bowl = Competition

3.    Quality of the water in the bowl = Business Environment / Economy

4.    First 120 Days of Life = Start-up

5.    Genetic make-up = Differentiation

Assuming you've already been in business for four months, the only thing you can control is how you differentiate yourself. How you stand out in a "sea of sameness."

## #7. Blue Ocean vs. Purple Goldfish Strategy

Purple Goldfish Strategy is "differentiation via added value." Finding signature extras that help you stand out, improve customer experience, reduce attrition, and drive positive word of mouth.

| RED OCEAN STRATEGY | PURPLE GOLDFISH STRATEGY | BLUE OCEAN STRATEGY |
|---|---|---|
| Compete in existing market space | Compete in existing market space, but stand out by giving little unexpected extras. | Create uncontested market space |
| Beat the competition | Differentiate yourself from the competition | Make the competition irrelevant |
| Exploit existing demand | Exploit current customer base to reduce attrition, drive loyalty, and promote word of mouth | Create and capture new demand |
| Make the value-cost trade-off | Break the transactional market economy mindset by adding value to exceed expectations | Break the value-cost trade-off |
| Align the whole system of a company's activities with its strategic choice of differentiation or low cost | Align the whole system of a company's activities in pursuit of differentiation through added value | Align the whole system of a company's activities in pursuit of differentiation and low cost |

## #8. Acts of Kindness

Think of lagniappe as an added branded act of kindness. A beacon or sign that shows you care. Marketing via G.L.U.E. (giving little unexpected extras). A little something thrown in for good measure.

| 1.0 RANDOM | 2.0 BRANDED | 3.0 LAGNIAPPE |
|---|---|---|
| Unpromoted | Promoted | Unexpected / Expected |
| Untargeted | Prospect + Customers | Customer-Focused |
| One-Off | Campaign | Everyday |
| Opportunistic | Planned | Ingrained |
| Relevant to the Recipient | Relevant to the Brand | Relevant to Brand + Recipient |
| In the Field | Near Point-of-Purchase | At Point-of-Purchase |
| PR Focused | PR + Brand | PR + Brand + CX + WOM |

## #9. Lagniappe Economy

There is a middle ground between a Market Economy (quid pro quo) and a Gift Economy (free). A lagniappe economy is where there is an exchange of goods and services for an exact value (market economy), plus a little unexpected extra that is given for good measure (gift economy).

## #10. v4 Principle

v4 is when a consumer becomes a PROsumer. They stand up for a product or service and vouch for it, giving personal assurances to its value. As a marketer you need to figure out a way to make your product or service remark-able. Are you giving your customers something to talk, tweet, blog, and post to Facebook about?

## #11. Lagniappe Takeaway: Creating Sales Lift

This is probably the most exciting takeaway. Giving a Purple Goldfish can increase your sales. Research from the International Journal of Marketing Studies has revealed that giving a gift before purchase could increase consumer spending by over 40%.

## PART TWO: TEN TYPES OF PURPLE GOLDFISH

Are you doing the little things for your customers? There are ten impactful ways you can provide little extras.

| VALUE | MAINTENANCE |
|---|---|
| #1 Throw-Ins | #6 Added Service |
| #2 Sampling | #7 Convenience |
| #3 Guarantees | #8 Waiting |
| #4 Pay it Forward | #9 Handling Mistakes |
| #5 First and Last Impressions | #10 Follow-Up |

Half are based on "value" and half are based on "maintenance" according to the value/maintenance matrix:

## VALUE

The "what" and "when" of customer experience:

- What are the tangible and intangible benefits that your service or product provides?

- Does your product or service go above and beyond to exceed customer expectations?

- Are you giving that little unexpected extra to surprise and delight your customer?

The first five types of Purple Goldfish seek to increase value for the customer. They include:

**#1. Throw-ins** – little extras that are included with your product or service. They help you stand out in a sea of sameness:

Example: "Bags Fly Free" and no change fees on Southwest.

**#2. Sampling** – little extras that give your customer an additional taste by offering a free something extra on the house.

Example: Order a box of tea from Bigelow Tea and you'll be treated to a sample of another flavor on the house.

**#3. Guarantees** – giving your customers that little extra pledge that you'll stand behind your product or service.

Example: Jansport backpacks are backed up … for life.

**#4. Pay it Forward** – give a little extra back to the community.

Example: If you are out of work and need a suit cleaned for an interview, Plaza Cleaners will clean it for free.

**#5. First and Last Impressions** – little extras that make you memorable and, more importantly, talk-able. You have two chances to make an impression—when your customer comes through the "door" and right before they walk out, hang up, or log off.

Example: Sample a Gibson guitar at Hard Rock Hotels. Check in, plug-in, and rock out.

# MAINTENANCE

Maintenance focuses on the who and how of the customer experience.

- What is the buying experience like for your customer?

- Do you make things turnkey or simple for your customer?

- Are you responsive to problems/issues for your customer?

The second five types of Purple Goldfish seek to reduce maintenance for the customer.

They include:

**#6. Added Service** – the little extra that's an added unexpected service.

Example: Safelite repairs or replaces your auto glass, and they also vacuum your car and clean your windows.

**#7. Convenience** – the little extras you add to make things easier for your customers.

Example: Most TD Bank locations are open seven days a week and some nights until 8 p.m.

**#8. Waiting** – the little extra to make waiting more bearable, especially if waiting is inevitable.

Example: Pacific Cafe gives you a glass of wine on the house to enjoy while you wait for your table.

**#9. Handling Mistakes** – admitting that you're wrong and doing the little extra above and beyond to make it more than right.

Example: Panera corrects their mistake and then gives you a free bakery treat to apologize.

**#10. Follow-up** – make the little extra follow-up with your customer.

Example: Rite Aid follows up with a call to check on a patient.

## TWO STORIES

At the age of 16 David McConnell started to sell books door-to-door in upstate New York. When his fare was not well received, McConnell resorted to a little lagniappe. David would promise a free gift—a vial of perfume—in exchange for being allowed to make a sales pitch. McConnell soon learned his customers adored his perfume, yet remained indifferent to his books. He then started the California Perfume Company that would become Avon Cosmetics in 1886. Today, despite competition from hundreds of American and foreign brand name cosmetics, Avon is #1 in sales nationwide, with Avon Ladies ringing doorbells coast to coast.

The second story is about a company founded by a social worker and a psychologist. Without the capital to open a restaurant, Stacy Madison and Mark Andrus began serving healthy pita bread roll-up sandwiches in Boston's Financial District. Their lunch cart was popular and soon lines started to form around the block. To make waiting more palatable (literally), Stacy concocted a lagniappe for customers waiting in line. Each night they baked the leftover pita bread sprinkled with seasoning to create flavored chips, which were a huge hit. Soon Stacy's Pita Chip Company was born. Stacy's experienced rapid growth, doubling sales every year which led to a multi-million dollar acquisition by Frito Lay in 2005.

## THE PURPLE GOLDFISH BACKSTORY

Stan Phelps first learned of the concept 'lagniappe' in 2003. The idea of merchants giving a little something extra clicked for him and he started looking for examples in the world of marketing, hence 'marketing lagniappe': any time a business purposely goes above and beyond to provide a little something extra. In 2009, he launched the Purple Goldfish Project with the goal of crowd-sourcing 1,001 examples of marketing lagniappe. Note: see the Resources section for a link to the outcome of the Purple Goldfish Project.

The first edition of *What's Your Purple Goldfish?* was published in 2012. It shares the concepts behind customer experience and examples of how some of our favorite companies go above and beyond. The second edition, *Purple Goldfish 2.0*, was published in 2019. It adds new examples and introduces the I.D.E.A. process to create a Purple Goldfish of your own.

### What is a Purple Goldfish?

Purple Goldfish is the concept of taking better care of your current customers by going above and beyond to provide exceptional customer experience by giving them that little unexpected extra. Purple Goldfish are those little unexpected extras. It's an investment into your customer base to achieve product differentiation, drive retention, and promote word of mouth.

 The biggest myth in marketing is the idea of meeting expectations. There is no such thing as meeting expectations. You either exceed them or you fall short. In a world where **60-80 percent** of customers describe themselves as satisfied or very satisfied before going on to defect to other brands, merely "meeting expectations" is no longer an option.

Many of your favorite companies use Purple Goldfish, whether they use the term or not: Five Guy's gives extra "bonus fries" in the bag and ballpark peanuts while you wait. Izzy's Ice Cream has the little scoop or "Izzy" added to the top of each cone. Safelight unexpectedly details your car while the windshield resin dries. Nurse Next Door delivers a warm apple pie when they've made a mistake. All of these examples embrace the concept of G.L.U.E. or Giving Little Unexpected Extras.

EXERCISE 1

# IDENTIFY A PURPLE GOLDFISH IN THE WILD

Think about your favorite companies, the ones that exceed your expectations and make it clear that they really care about you. What are their Purple Goldfish? Think of a Purple Goldfish you've encountered in the wild and how it aligns with the concept of G.L.U.E. Write your answers below to share with the group.

## Describe a Purple Goldfish from One of Your Favorite Companies:

COMPANY

THEIR PURPLE GOLDFISH

WHY IT STANDS OUT TO YOU:

## What are your company's Purple Goldfish? Write your answers below to share with the group.

EXAMPLE PURPLE GOLDFISH
# ZANE'S CYCLES

Zane's Cycles is a Purple Goldfish Hall of Fame company. The company is built on customer service as a point of differentiation. A veteran of the retail bicycle industry for more than three decades, founder Chris Zane has built the Branford, Connecticut, business into one of the largest bicycle stores in the nation by giving customers more than they expect. More importantly, they stand behind the sale by giving more service than is reasonably expected (especially by competitors). Here are 10 compelling ways that Zane's offers little extras to maximize lifetime value and reduce maintenance:

**Throw-ins (value): Gift Certificates in Water Bottles** – Buy a gift certificate and Zane's will throw in a complimentary branded water bottle to hold the certificate.

**Sampling (value): 30-Day Test Ride** – Purchasing a new bike can be overwhelming, especially when many bikes feel similar. Then there are the many color options and component groups to select from at Zane's. Their goal is "to do our very best to get you on the bike of your dreams but sometimes you don't know if the bike you purchased is the right fit for you until you get out and ride. To make sure that you have purchased the correct bicycle, ride it for 30 days. If during that time you are not completely satisfied, please return the bicycle for an exchange. We will gladly give a full credit toward your new selection."

**Guarantees (value): Lifetime Service** – Every bicycle purchased from Zane's Cycles comes with their exclusive Zane's Cycles Lifetime Free Service and Parts Warranty. Anytime your bicycle needs a service, a full-tune up, or just a quick adjustment, Zane's will make those necessary adjustments for free as long as you own your bicycle.

**Paying it Forward (value): Wishing Wheels** – At the Wishing Wheels Holiday Bike Drive folks work together to assemble the many bikes that were purchased with Roots4Relief fund drive dollars over the course of five weeks. The assembled bikes then go to children in need. In 2018, Zane's was able to assemble and donate nearly 200 bikes!

**First / Last Impressions (value): Test Rides** – Want to test a bike at Zane's? You're free to take it out for a ride. No credit card or driver's license required. Each year they lose a handful of bikes, but the small cost is insignificant compared to the trust gained and hassle avoided.

**Added Service (maintenance): Free Trade-in Program for Kids** – Buy a bike for your child at Zane's. When they outgrow it, simply bring it back to trade-up. Zane's gives you a credit for the price of the former bike toward a new one.

**Convenience (maintenance): Webcam** – Zane's has a camera in the repair shop which gives customers the ability to Skype the team at work.

**Waiting (maintenance): Coffee Bar** – Zane's has a nice espresso bar in the store that encourages customers to relax and enjoy a cup of gourmet coffee while shopping.

**Handling Mistakes (maintenance) Founder's Promise** – Zane's is committed to service and getting it right. You can find this message on its website: "If you don't feel that we are living up to our mission, let us know and we'll fix it immediately. If you have a concern and would like to discuss it with me, Chris Zane, directly, please e-mail me. I will personally respond to you."

**Follow-up (maintenance): Personal Notes** – each person who buys a bike from Zane's receives a handwritten thank you note.

## CUSTOMER EXPERIENCE AND WHY IT'S IMPORTANT

Investments in Customer Experience are justified by the return they provide in terms of customer loyalty (increased sales from one customer) and customer advocacy (new customers via referrals).

Financially speaking, this concept is called Customer Lifetime Value or LTV. That is, how much profit will we make from this customer, not just from one transaction, but from all future transactions. In addition to LTV, we believe its important to evaluate a customer's Referral Impact as well. That is, how much business is won or lost because of their positive or negative word-of-mouth.

Companies that fail to meet expectations often lose the customer and create negative word-of-mouth. In terms of Net Promoter Score or NPS, which you'll learn more about, these are Detractors. Companies that try to meet expectations usually fall short, losing the customer but often avoiding negative word-of-mouth. In terms of NPS, these are Passives. Companies that exceed expectations win customers for life and generate positive word-of-mouth and subsequent referrals. In terms of NPS, these are Promoters. As such, Detractors often have negative LTV, Passives have low LTV, and Promoters have high LTV.

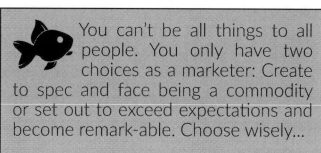

You can't be all things to all people. You only have two choices as a marketer: Create to spec and face being a commodity or set out to exceed expectations and become remark-able. Choose wisely...

**EXERCISE 2**

# CUSTOMER LIFETIME VALUE

Consider the tale of these three companies and just one of their customers. Each company treats the customer differently and this affects LTV.

**Company One:** A customer purchases $100 in products, for a net profit of $40. The customer is dissatisfied and tells five people about her poor experience. They lose two loyal customers that year and the original customer doesn't return again.

**Company Two:** A customer purchases $100 in products, for a net profit of $40. The customer received what she ordered, but didn't enjoy the experience of doing business with the company. She doesn't tell anyone about her experience and she also doesn't return.

**Company Three:** A customer purchases $100 in products, for a gross profit of $40. The company spends an extra $10 on Purple Goldfish, making the net profit $30. The customer is delighted and tells five people about her great experience. During the next year, the customer returns twice and the company gains two new customers.

**Calculate the lifetime value and referral impact for a customer at each company:**

| | | COMPANY ONE | COMPANY TWO | COMPANY THREE |
|---|---|---|---|---|
| **FIRST SALE** | +/- Profit | $40 | $40 | $30 |
| **REFERRAL IMPACT** | +/- Profit | $-40 | $0 | $30 |
| | x Customers | 2 | | 2 |
| | Subtotal | $-80 | | $60 |
| **RETURN VISITS** | +/- Profit | $0 | $0 | $30 |
| | x Visits | | | 2 |
| | Subtotal | | | $60 |
| **TOTAL LTV + REFERRAL IMPACT** | | $-40 | $40 | $150 |

## ACTS OF KINDNESS

Acts of kindness come in many forms. All are signs that you care about a customer, but not all qualify as lagniappe. Let's explore the differences.

**1.0 Random Acts of Kindness:** Good deeds or unexpected acts. They are usually one-off, feel-good activations. A random act of kindness draws upon gift economy principles with no expectation of immediate return, with the exception of possible PR value.

EXAMPLE

**2.0 Branded Acts of Kindness:** Here the item given is usually tied closely with the brand and its positioning. It's less random, more planned, and potentially a series of activations. This has the feel of a traditional marketing campaign.

EXAMPLE

**3.0 Lagniape Acts of Kindness:** Kindness that is imbedded into your brand. Rooted in the idea of "added value" to the transaction. Not a one- off or a campaign, but an everyday practice that's focused on customers of your brand.

EXAMPLE

| 1.0 RANDOM | 2.0 BRANDED | 3.0 LAGNIAPPE |
|---|---|---|
| Unpromoted | Promoted | Unexpected / Expected |
| Untargeted | Prospect + Customers | Customer-Focused |
| One-Off | Campaign | Everyday |
| Opportunistic | Planned | Ingrained |
| Relevant to the Recipient | Relevant to the Brand | Relevant to Brand + Recipient |
| In the Field | Near Point-of-Purchase | At Point-of-Purchase |
| PR Focused | PR + Brand | PR + Brand + CX + WOM |

## NOTES

Implementing a Purple Goldfish Strategy involves the following key concepts:

## Growth is Determined by Five Factors

The growth of your product or service is similar to that of a goldfish. Growth is determined by five factors:

1. **Size of the bowl** = _____

2. **Number of other goldfish in the bowl** = _____

3. **Quality of the water in the bowl or pond** = _____

4. **First 120 days of life** = _____

5. **Genetic make-up** = _____

Assuming you've already been in business for four months, the only thing you can control is how you differentiate yourself. How you stand out in a sea of sameness?

## Differentiation

Differentiation is how your company stands out from others in the marketplace. These differences create unique meaning for your brand and determines how you are separated from others. Differentiation is key in marketing. In the words of the late Harvard Business School professor Ted Levitt, "The search for meaningful distinction is central to the marketing effort. If marketing is about anything, it is about achieving customer-getting distinction by differentiating what you do and how you operate. All else is derivative of that and only that."

## Personas

A buyer persona is a fictional representation of your ideal customer based on market research and real data about your existing customers. Customer personas allow you to step into the customers shoes, understand your offerings, and see the customer experience from their perspective. Personas should be based upon research, validated through customer feedback, and segmented across different customer types. When accurate and used effectively, personas ensures you're designing customer experience solutions that meet customer needs. In order to identify which Purple Goldfish will be most successful, you need to understand your customer and their experience.

## Journey Mapping

Journey maps are a tool to help you understand the process your customer goes through before, during, and after their transaction. By mapping the five stages of the customer journey, you can understand what their experience is. A journey map can help you identify the places where the experience breaks down, where it can be improved, and where you can add Purple Goldfish.

## Touchpoints

Touchpoints are the set of activities a customer is involved with before, during, and after a transaction with a company.

## Gaps and Opportunities

Gaps and opportunities are points along your customer journey that are either, 1. a source of frustration for your customers or 2. a chance to delight them with and elevated peak experience.

EXERCISE 3
# THE R.U.L.E.S.

There are five ingredients or R.U.L.E.S. when creating a Purple Goldfish:

- Relevant - it should be of value to the recipient

- Unexpected - it should "surprise and delight"

- Limited - it should be something rare, hard to find or signature to your business

- Expressive - it should be a sign that you care

- Sticky - it should be memorable and talkable

**Think back to the Purple Goldfish you identified from one of your favorite companies. Does it follow the R.U.L.E.S.?**

| WAS IT... | YES/NO | HOW SO? OR WHY NOT? |
|-----------|--------|---------------------|
| Relevant | | |
| Unexpected | | |
| Limited | | |
| Expressive | | |
| Sticky | | |

EXERCISE 4

# THE VALUE/MAINTENANCE MATRIX

**Value:** the what and when of customer experience

- What are the tangible and intangible benefits that your service or product provides?

- Does your product or service go above and beyond to exceed customer expectations?

- What is a little unexpected extra that surprises and delights?

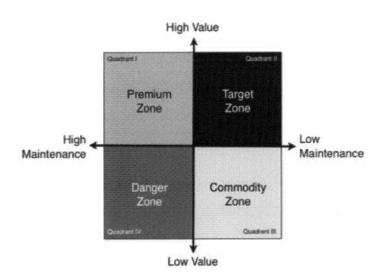

**Maintenance**: the who and how of customer experience

- What is the buying experience like for your customer?

- Do you make things turnkey or simple for your customer?

- Are you responsive to problems/issues for your customer?

**Think about the Purple Goldfish you identified from one of your favorite companies. Was it based on value or maintenance?**

☐ VALUE ☐ MAINTENANCE

WHAT INFLUENCED YOUR DECISION?

_____

_____

_____

# NOTES

# 3. INQUIRE

## THE I IN THE I.D.E.A. PROCESS

Using the I.D.E.A. Process to create your own Purple Goldfish begins with the Inquire phase. In this phase you will:

- Find out what's important to your customers.

- Create journey maps of your customers' experience.

- Identify what gaps and opportunities exist in your current customer journey.

### Get Insights from Customer Personas and Proto-Personas

If you walked around most successful companies and asked employees to describe their customers, you'll hear many different answers. However, if you asked executives if they understand their customers, the answer will always be a resounding "yes." Most companies believe they understand their customers, but without a customer persona they have no way of knowing if everyone is on the same page or not.

Customer personas allow you to step into the customers shoes, understanding your offerings and customer experience from their perspective. Personas should be based upon research, validated through customer feedback, and segmented across different customer types. When accurate and used effectively, personas ensure you're designing customer experience solutions that meet customer needs.

# AN EXAMPLE PROTO-PERSONA

Personas are profiles of prototypical customers, based on data from actual customers. Proto-personas are like personas, but instead of being based on data, they're based on your personal experiences and knowledge of your existing customers.

Here is an fictitious example of a proto-persona for a Zane's Cycles customer.

| WHO AM I? | | AUDIENCE SEGMENT | |
|---|---|---|---|
| Name: Steve Smith<br><br>Profession: Financial Advisor    Age: 34 | | Weekend Warrior | |
| **THREE THINGS THAT ARE IMPORTANT TO ME** | | **THREE THINGS THAT ARE NOT IMPORTANT TO ME** | |
| 1 Diverse selection of bikes<br><br>2 Staff knowledgable about training bikes<br><br>3 Convenient location near my house | | 1 Not that sensitive to price<br><br>2 Online reviews<br><br>3 No brand sensitivity | |
| MY INTERESTS | MY PERSONALITY | MY SKILLS | MY DESIRES |
| Outdoor enthusiast, foodie, likes live music | Competitive, driven, likes to host gatherings | Financial analysis, well-spoken, can play guitar | Want to push myself physically and mentally. Wishes to give back to the community. |

## EXERCISE 5
# CREATE A PROTO-PERSONA

To give you a taste of creating a customer persona, you will create a proto-persona. After the workshop, you can then use this proto-persona as a starting point for building out full, research-based personas of your customers and audience segments.

**Fill in the blanks below for one of your own audience segments.**

| WHO AM I? | | AUDIENCE SEGMENT | |
|---|---|---|---|
| Name: <br> Profession:                    Age: | | | |
| **THREE THINGS THAT ARE IMPORTANT TO ME** | | **THREE THINGS THAT ARE NOT IMPORTANT TO ME** | |
| 1 <br><br> 2 <br><br> 3 | | 1 <br><br> 2 <br><br> 3 | |
| MY INTERESTS | MY PERSONALITY | MY SKILLS | MY DESIRES |
| | | | |

EXERCISE 6

# CREATE AN ATTRIBUTE MAP

Once you have personas or proto-personas, you can assess how well you perform against their desires by creating an Attribute Map: a graph that lists your customer's needs on one side and your rating of your relative performance on a scale of 1 to 5.

**Step One:** What are the top six things your customers value when evaluating your product or service? These six factors are your attributes.

1. _____

2. _____

3. _____

4. _____

5. _____

6. _____

**Step Two:** Rank the six attributes below from most important to least important.

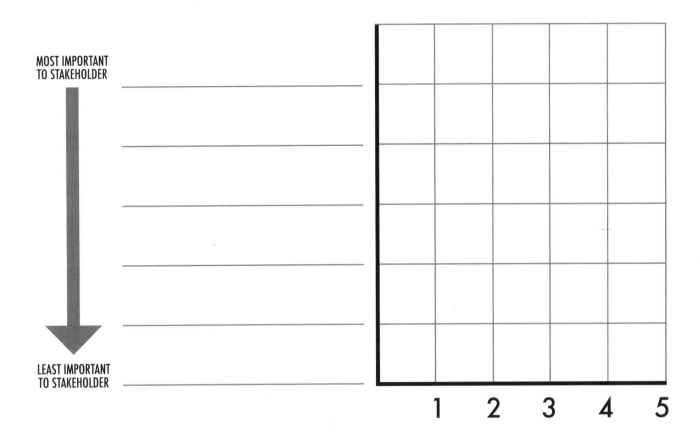

MOST IMPORTANT
TO STAKEHOLDER

LEAST IMPORTANT
TO STAKEHOLDER

1   2   3   4   5

**Step Three:** Use the initial of your company and grade your performance for each attribute on the graph above. Five is best and one is worst.

**Step Four:** Use the initials of your top two competitors and rank them on the attributes as well.

# JOURNEY MAPPING

Every customer's journey is unique but often share similar steps or touchpoints. Especially within one customer segment, much can be learned by creating a journey map for a typical customer in that segment.

Journey maps help you understand these similarities and design experiences that deliver the right value at the right time for the customer.

There are many types of journey maps. For our work together we'll cover a current state journey map. Our goal is to capture what often happens for today's customers, rather than what we believe should happen.

Every interaction a customer has with you before, during, and after their purchase is a touchpoint. When these touchpoints are listed sequentially, you now have a journey map.

In our I.D.E.A. Process, we will evaluate each touchpoint in the customer journey, identify gaps and opportunities in the customer experience, and use those insights to create Purple Goldfish.

For now, let's dive into a journey map example.

## NOTES

# EXAMPLE JOURNEY MAP

|  | AWARE | CONSIDER |
|---|---|---|
| **WEB/MOBILE** | Sees an ad for Zane's Cycles while signing up for the triathlon <br><br> ☐ GAP <br> ☐ OPP | Searches zanes.com and reviews selection of bikes <br><br> ☒ GAP <br> ☐ OPP |
| **TRADE SHOW/ EVENTS** | Went to race expo with a friend and saw a booth from Zane's where they were doing free tune-ups <br><br> ☐ GAP <br> ☐ OPP | ☐ GAP <br> ☐ OPP |
| **ADVERTISING** | Comes across a half-page ad for Zane's in the sports section of the local newspaper <br><br> ☐ GAP <br> ☐ OPP | ☐ GAP <br> ☐ OPP |
| **SOCIAL MEDIA** | ☐ GAP <br> ☐ OPP | Posts on Facebook and asks friends for recommendations on where to buy a training bike <br><br> ☒ GAP <br> ☐ OPP |
| **WORD OF MOUTH** | ☐ GAP <br> ☐ OPP | Asked friends during a training run about the best bike to buy <br><br> ☐ GAP <br> ☐ OPP |
| **IN STORE** | ☐ GAP <br> ☐ OPP | ☐ GAP <br> ☐ OPP |

**Starting Point:** Deciding to Purchase a New Bike

**Audience Segment:** Weekend Warrior

| BUY | USE | SHARE |
|---|---|---|
| Received receipt from the store. Will receive text/email when the bike is ready for pick-up ☐ GAP ☐ OPP | ☐ GAP ☐ OPP | Writes a Google review for Zane's ☐ GAP ☐ OPP |
| ☐ GAP ☐ OPP | Use bike for training and compete in the local triathlon ☐ GAP ☒ OPP | ☐ GAP ☐ OPP |
| ☐ GAP ☐ OPP | ☐ GAP ☐ OPP | ☐ GAP ☐ OPP |
| ☐ GAP ☐ OPP | Shares picture on bike from the triathlon. It has a Zane's sticker on it ☐ GAP ☐ OPP | ☐ GAP ☐ OPP |
| ☐ GAP ☐ OPP | ☐ GAP ☐ OPP | Shares feedback with friends on how easy it was to shop at Zane's ☐ GAP ☐ OPP |
| Went into the Zane's Cyles store, got fitted and ordered the bike ☐ GAP ☒ OPP | Brings bike in for a tune-up after the race and takes advantage of lifetime service ☐ GAP ☐ OPP | ☐ GAP ☐ OPP |

EXERCISE 7

# CREATE YOUR OWN JOURNEY MAP

| | AWARE | CONSIDER |
|---|---|---|
| **WEB/MOBILE** | ☐ GAP<br>☐ OPP | ☐ GAP<br>☐ OPP |
| **TRADE SHOW/ EVENTS** | ☐ GAP<br>☐ OPP | ☐ GAP<br>☐ OPP |
| **ADVERTISING** | ☐ GAP<br>☐ OPP | ☐ GAP<br>☐ OPP |
| **SOCIAL MEDIA** | ☐ GAP<br>☐ OPP | ☐ GAP<br>☐ OPP |
| **WORD OF MOUTH** | ☐ GAP<br>☐ OPP | ☐ GAP<br>☐ OPP |
| **IN STORE** | ☐ GAP<br>☐ OPP | ☐ GAP<br>☐ OPP |

**Starting Point:** _____

**Audience Segment:** _____

| BUY | USE | SHARE |
|---|---|---|
| ☐ GAP<br>☐ OPP | ☐ GAP<br>☐ OPP | ☐ GAP<br>☐ OPP |
| ☐ GAP<br>☐ OPP | ☐ GAP<br>☐ OPP | ☐ GAP<br>☐ OPP |
| ☐ GAP<br>☐ OPP | ☐ GAP<br>☐ OPP | ☐ GAP<br>☐ OPP |
| ☐ GAP<br>☐ OPP | ☐ GAP<br>☐ OPP | ☐ GAP<br>☐ OPP |
| ☐ GAP<br>☐ OPP | ☐ GAP<br>☐ OPP | ☐ GAP<br>☐ OPP |
| ☐ GAP<br>☐ OPP | ☐ GAP<br>☐ OPP | ☐ GAP<br>☐ OPP |

# GAPS AND OPPORTUNITIES

A gap in your customer journey is a point at which your business processes get in the way of your customer's goal. Opportunities are points at which you can create a peak experience.

If you look back at the example journey map on page 28 and 29, you'll notice some touchpoints are marked as gaps or opportunities. Here's a list of those gaps and opportunities.

| GAPS | OPPORTUNITIES |
| --- | --- |
| Customers can't find the information they need about products when using a mobile device<br><br>Customers aren't sure where to go for advice or feedback | Getting a new bike is a proud moment, perhaps one we should help the customer celebrate<br><br>Beginners can easily be overwhelmed, so what can we do to help? |

Next you will review your own journey map and make note of the potential gaps and opportunities.

## EXERCISE 8
# IDENTIFYING GAPS AND OPPORTUNITIES

Step One: Return to your journey map on pages 30 and 31, read through each touchpoint and ask the following questions:

At this touchpoint have we...

- fully addressed the customer's needs?

- provided as much value as possible to the customer?

- fully eliminated friction from the process?

- created more work for the customer than necessary?

As you answer those questions, gaps and opportunities will be come obvious to you. Remember, gaps are points where your business opportunities get in the way and opportunities are points where you can go above and beyond to create a peak experience for the customer.

Once you mark up your journey map, return to this page and list the gaps and oppotunities you identified. The list will come in handy as we move forward.

| GAPS | OPPORTUNITIES |
|------|---------------|
|      |               |

## THE D IN THE I.D.E.A. PROCESS

With your customer's journey mapped and the gaps and opportunities identified, you can now set your focus to choosing which ones to address and generating ideas for doing just that in the Design phase.

Before beginning Design, it's important to adopt the right mindset. Our focus during design isn't to evaluate the ideas we generate. Rather, our focus should be on generating as many ideas as possible.

## DESIGN THINKING EXERCISE

**In the box below draw a vase of flowers.**

## WHICH GAPS ARE MOST DAMAGING?

A good place to start the design process is to focus on the gaps that are most damaging to your customer experience.

For our prototypical example from Zane's Cycles, here's our list:

| OUR TOP FIVE GAPS |
| --- |
| 1. Mobile site isn't responsive |
| 2. Online sellers offer lower prices |
| 3. Need to keep customers active in Zane's community |
| 4. Gap between getting fitted and bike delivered |
| 5. Staff turnover |

We identified these gaps by asking a few questions.

After which gaps do we tend to...

- lose the most customers?

- see NPS or other performance measures drop?

- receive the most customer complaints?

Now it is your turn to identify your top five gaps.

## EXERCISE 9

# FOCUS ON YOUR MOST DAMAGING GAPS

Use the space below to list your top five most damaging gaps. If you have access to data to help you rank the gaps, feel free to use it. If not, imagine you are the customer. Which of the gaps would feel the most egregious to you? Remember the list of questions above to help you make your list.

| YOUR TOP FIVE GAPS |
|---|
| 1. |
| 2. |
| 3. |
| 4. |
| 5. |

# WHICH OPPORTUNITIES ARE MOST PROMISING?

Opportunities are bit more challenging than gaps. While it may seem obvious which gaps are most damaging, it requires more imagination to select the most promising opportunities.

For our prototypical example from Zane's Cycles, here's our list:

| OUR TOP FIVE OPPORTUNITIES |
|---|
| 1. Getting people to be aware of lifetime service |
| 2. We have a huge selection of bikes |
| 3. Unique trade-in program for kids bikes |
| 4. Supporter of the bike community |
| 5. Knowledgeable staff who are bikers |

We identified these opportunities by asking a few questions.

Which opportunities...

- are directly related to our core product or service?

- are most important to our target customers?

- will serve the majority of our customers or prospects?

- will create competitive separation in the marketplace?

- are unlike anything we've done before?

Now it is your turn to identify your top five opportunities.

EXERCISE 10

# FOCUS ON YOUR MOST PROMISING OPPORTUNITIES

Use the space below to list your top five most promising opportunities. As you make the list, remember the list of questions on the previous page. Don't forget to put yourself in the customer's shoes. Which opportunities, might become a great touchpoint to surprise and delight?

| YOUR TOP FIVE OPPORTUNITIES |
| --- |
| 1. |
| 2. |
| 3. |
| 4. |
| 5. |

## ASK BIG QUESTIONS

Now that you know your top five gaps and opportunities, it's time to generate ideas for your own Purple Goldfish. At this stage, we call them PGF's, which is short for Purple Goldfish Fry. Fry, of course, being the name for a baby goldfish.

You will spend time brainstorming PGF's to address each gap and opportunity on your focused list.

We called this section "Ask Big Questions" and now that we're set up to brainstorm, we finally get to ask those big questions. We find that it's helpful to ask thought-provoking questions around each gap or opportunity to elicit different ideas to address them. Here's our go-to list of questions:

- If it were magic, how would it happen?

- If we eliminated x altogether, what could we replace it with?

- What is the confusing part about x?

- How have others solved x?

- If you had a budget of one million dollars, how would you solve this problem? What about a budget of ten dollars?

- If you had a year to solve this problem, how would you do it? What if you had ten minutes?

You will likely develop some of your own questions as well. We like questions that go to the extremes, as you can see with the last two questions focused on budget and timeline. Often times the best ideas come from the pared back version of a much larger, but infeasible idea. Those questions help develop those big ideas.

# EXAMPLE

When we asked the big questions for one of the gaps and one of the opportunities for Zane's Cycles, here's what we came up with:

---

GAP: Customers can't find the information they need when using a mobile device

IDEAS: Consider a responsive design

Create a mobile app

Improve search

Offer online chat

Produce short, mobile-friendly videos

---

OPPORTUNITY: Support the bike community with robust offerings

IDEAS: Organize training rides

Put on local workshops

Create a training calculator

Celebrate customer's race wins

Create a group for owners on Facebook

---

EXERCISE 11

# BRAINSTORM IDEAS TO ADDRESS GAPS

We'll start by brainstorming ideas to address your gaps. Spend time asking the questions from page 39 for each of your gaps and make notes in the space provided.

GAP #1:

IDEAS:

GAP #2:

IDEAS:

GAP #3: _____

IDEAS: _____

_____

_____

_____

_____

_____

_____


GAP #4: _____

IDEAS: _____

_____

_____

_____

_____

_____

_____

GAP #5:

IDEAS:

Use this extra space for additional notes while you brainstorm.

EXERCISE 12

# BRAINSTORM IDEAS TO ADDRESS OPPORTUNITIES

Now that we've worked through your gaps, let's work on opportunities. Spend time asking the questions from page 39 for each of your opportunities and make notes in the space provided.

OPPORTUNITY #1:

IDEAS:

OPPORTUNITY #2:

IDEAS:

OPPORTUNITY #3:

IDEAS:

OPPORTUNITY #4:

IDEAS:

OPPORTUNITY #5: _____

IDEAS: _____

_____

_____

_____

_____

_____

_____

Use this extra space for additional notes while you brainstorm.

## EXERCISE 12

# YOUR PGF'S

Now that you have a list of ideas for each of your gaps and opportunities, take some time to refine each of the ideas into a more formal PGF with a title and short description. This list will be what we use going forward into the Evaluate and Advance stages.

TITLE: ☐ GAP
☐ OPP

DESCRIPTION:

TITLE: ☐ GAP
☐ OPP

DESCRIPTION:

TITLE:

☐ GAP
☐ OPP

DESCRIPTION:

TITLE:

☐ GAP
☐ OPP

DESCRIPTION:

TITLE:

☐ GAP
☐ OPP

DESCRIPTION:

TITLE:

☐ GAP
☐ OPP

DESCRIPTION:

TITLE:

☐ GAP
☐ OPP

DESCRIPTION:

---

TITLE:

☐ GAP
☐ OPP

DESCRIPTION:

---

TITLE:

☐ GAP
☐ OPP

DESCRIPTION:

---

TITLE:

☐ GAP
☐ OPP

DESCRIPTION:

## NOTES

## THE E IN THE I.D.E.A. PROCESS

The Evaluate phase is where you assess the feasibility and validity of the potential Purple Goldfish—your PGF's—from both internal and external perspectives.

Evaluation is a three-step process, including Internal Evaluation, External Validation, and Pilot. While it's often not possible to complete these steps throughly in a workshop setting, we will create a plan for each.

### EXERCISE 13
## INTERNAL EVALUATION QUESTIONS

To evaluate your PGF's, answer these questions:

- What resources will be needed to implement this idea?

- What are the costs associated with those resources?

- If you're successful, how many of your current customers are likely to take advantage of this Purple Goldfish? Do you expect increased loyalty from these customers?

- If you're successful, how many new customers do you expect this Purple Goldfish may attract?

- Can you expect benefits beyond additional sales and loyalty?

- Are there any intangible benefits?

- Do the costs outweigh the benefits?

Once you answer these questions for each PGF, you'll then make a go or no-go decision to move the PGF to the next step, which is External Validation.

# INTERNAL EVALUATION QUESTIONS

Use this grid to record answers to the internal evaluation questions on page 51.

| YOUR PGF | WHAT RESOURCES ARE NEEDED? | WHAT ARE THE ASSOCIATED COSTS? |
|---|---|---|
|  |  |  |
|  |  |  |
|  |  |  |
|  |  |  |
|  |  |  |

| WHAT BENEFITS CAN WE EXPECT? LOYALTY? NEW CUSTOMERS? ADDITIONAL TANGIBLE AND INTANGIBLE BENEFITS? | DO THE COSTS OUTWEIGH BENEFITS? | READY FOR EXTERNAL VALIDATION? |
|---|---|---|
| | ☐ YES ☐ NO | ☐ YES ☐ NO |
| | ☐ YES ☐ NO | ☐ YES ☐ NO |
| | ☐ YES ☐ NO | ☐ YES ☐ NO |
| | ☐ YES ☐ NO | ☐ YES ☐ NO |
| | ☐ YES ☐ NO | ☐ YES ☐ NO |

# INTERNAL EVALUATION QUESTIONS

Use this grid to record answers to the internal evaluation questions on page 51.

| YOUR PGF | WHAT RESOURCES ARE NEEDED? | WHAT ARE THE ASSOCIATED COSTS? |
|---|---|---|
| | | |
| | | |
| | | |
| | | |
| | | |

# 5. EVALUATE

| WHAT BENEFITS CAN WE EXPECT? LOYALTY? NEW CUSTOMERS? ADDITIONAL TANGIBLE AND INTANGIBLE BENEFITS? | DO THE COSTS OUTWEIGH BENEFITS? | READY FOR EXTERNAL VALIDATION? |
|---|---|---|
| | ☐ YES ☐ NO | ☐ YES ☐ NO |
| | ☐ YES ☐ NO | ☐ YES ☐ NO |
| | ☐ YES ☐ NO | ☐ YES ☐ NO |
| | ☐ YES ☐ NO | ☐ YES ☐ NO |
| | ☐ YES ☐ NO | ☐ YES ☐ NO |

**EXERCISE 14**
# EXTERNAL VALIDATION

Before initiating the Pilot phase, get input from customers that you're heading in the right direction. We recommend some of the following methods for getting customer input:

- Focus groups

- Customer advisory board meetings

- Surveys

- One-on-one customer interviews

Of course, most of these methods require advance planning. So we'll create a plan to gain the necessary insight. For the purposes of this exercise, and those going forward, pick your five most promising PGF's as your focus.

| YOUR PGF | WHAT DO YOU NEED TO LEARN FROM CUSTOMERS TO VALIDATE THE IDEA? | HOW WILL YOU GET THE INFORMATION YOU NEED? |
|---|---|---|
|  |  |  |
|  |  |  |
|  |  |  |
|  |  |  |
|  |  |  |

**EXERCISE 15**

# PLANNING YOUR PILOT

With internal evaluation and external validation completed, you're ready to pilot the selected PGF's. Of course, we won't be able to complete a pilot during the course of this workshop, but we can create a plan for the pilot.

Here are some tips we recommend you keep in mind as you put together your pilot:

- Make sure your pilot is sufficiently sized, by reach or timeframe, to generate a representative sample of your target customers.

- Build measurement into the process. As you are planning the pilot, you will want to determine how you'll measure the effects of the PGF. An uptick in sales would be marvelous, but sales may be a lagging indicator. Consider other ways to measure those customers or locations that are part of the Pilot relative to the rest of your customers.

- Engage in proper training for your team. Remember when outward-facing, it's not a "pilot," it's the new thing. You'll want your team to treat the PGF pilot as normally as possible to avoid skewed results or apathy toward the project.

- Listen to your team. To achieve buy-in and an effective launch, you'll also want to seek the feedback of your team members tasked with delivering your new PGF experience. This input will allow you to head off any opposition or issues that might interrupt an effective roll-out.

Of course, most of these methods require advance planning. So we'll create a plan to gain the necessary insight. For the purposes of this exercise, and those going forward, pick your five most promising PGF's as your focus.

## NOTES

# PLANNING YOUR PILOT

Use this grid to plan your pilot program for five of your PGF's. Use the notes on page 58 to help you complete the grid.

| YOUR PGF | HOW WILL YOU SELECT A SAMPLE OF CUSTOMERS? | HOW WILL YOU TRAIN YOUR TEAM? |
|---|---|---|
|  |  |  |
|  |  |  |
|  |  |  |
|  |  |  |
|  |  |  |

| HOW WILL YOU MEASURE THE RESULTS? | HOW WILL YOU SOLICIT F FEEDBACK FROM YOUR TEAM? | WHAT OTHER INFORMATION DO YOU NEED BEFORE ROLL OUT? |
|---|---|---|
| | | |
| | | |
| | | |
| | | |
| | | |

## THE LAST PHASE IN THE I.D.E.A. PROCESS

You're now ready to release your Purple Goldfish throughout your organization. To do this, you will need to:

- Achieve buy-in internally.

- Roll out the experience to customers.

- Set up a feedback loop with continuous measurement.

## COMPONENTS OF ACHIEVING BUY-IN

- Communicate the plan with the right stakeholders.

- Don't forget your front-line employees.

- Present the story of the idea.

- Use anecdotes to win hearts, data to win minds.

- Present adjustments based on pilot feedback

## ROLLOUT TIMELINES

You're now ready to apply Purple Goldfish strategies in your organization. Each strategy or plan requires a detailed description, specific measures of success, and resources.

| | |
|---|---|
| **First 30 Days** | Complete assessments. Determine current gaps and opportunities in your current customer experience. Outline measurement metrics. |
| **31 - 90 Days** | Put together a cross-functional design team. Generate ideas based on addressing current gaps and opportunities. Pressure test and force rank ideas for Pilots. Launch two or three pilots. |
| **91 - 180 Days** | Assess results from the Pilots. Achieve buy-in from leadership on ideas to advance throughout the organization. Determine resources, process, and training required to roll-out organization wide. Measure results. |

EXERCISE 16

## CREATING YOUR PLAN FOR ROLL OUT

The grid on the following two pages provides space to plan how you'll roll out your Purple Goldfish over the next 180 days and beyond. As you complete the plan, keep in mind the components of achieving buy-in and the suggested timeline above.

# YOUR ROLLOUT PLAN

| YOUR PURPLE GOLDFISH | 0-30 DAY PLAN | |
|---|---|---|
| | ACTIONS: | |
| | RESOURCES: | SUCCESS METRICS: |
| | ACTIONS: | |
| | RESOURCES: | SUCCESS METRICS: |
| | ACTIONS: | |
| | RESOURCES: | SUCCESS METRICS: |
| | ACTIONS: | |
| | RESOURCES: | SUCCESS METRICS: |
| | ACTIONS: | |
| | RESOURCES: | SUCCESS METRICS: |

| 31-90 DAY PLAN | | 91-180 DAY PLAN | |
| --- | --- | --- | --- |
| ACTIONS: | | ACTIONS: | |
| RESOURCES: | SUCCESS METRICS: | RESOURCES: | SUCCESS METRICS: |
| ACTIONS: | | ACTIONS: | |
| RESOURCES: | SUCCESS METRICS: | RESOURCES: | SUCCESS METRICS: |
| ACTIONS: | | ACTIONS: | |
| RESOURCES: | SUCCESS METRICS: | RESOURCES: | SUCCESS METRICS: |
| ACTIONS: | | ACTIONS: | |
| RESOURCES: | SUCCESS METRICS: | RESOURCES: | SUCCESS METRICS: |
| ACTIONS: | | ACTIONS: | |
| RESOURCES: | SUCCESS METRICS: | RESOURCES: | SUCCESS METRICS: |

## NOTES

## NOTES

## BASICS FIRST

Creating a Purple Goldfish is not a substitute for having a strong product or service. Get the basics right before considering the little unexpected extras.

## AUTHENTIC VS. FORCED

A Purple Goldfish is a beacon. A small gift or offering that demonstrates you care. It needs to be done in an authentic way. If it comes across as forced or contrived, you'll eliminate all of the goodwill and negatively impact your product or service.

## LIPOSUCTION?

Lagniappe is not a quick fix or for those seeking immediate results. Translation: it's not liposuction. It's equivalent to working out every day. The results gradually build and improve over time.

## IT'S A COMMITMENT, NOT A CAMPAIGN

A Purple Goldfish is different than a promotion or limited time offer. It's a feature that becomes embedded into the fabric of your product or service. Add one or a school of goldfish at your convenience, remove them at your peril.

## EVERY GREAT JOURNEY BEGINS WITH A SINGLE STEP

Start small when adding a signature extra and add gradually. The best brands are those who boast a whole school of Purple Goldfish.

## OTHER COLORS IN THE GOLDFISH SERIES

### GREEN GOLDFISH 2.0 – 15 KEYS TO DRIVING EMPLOYEE ENGAGEMENT

*Green Goldfish* is based on the simple premise that "happy engaged employees create happy enthused customers." The book focuses on 15 different ways to drive employee engagement and reinforce a strong corporate culture.

### GOLDEN GOLDFISH – THE VITAL FEW

*Golden Goldfish* examines the importance of your top 20 percent of customers and employees. The book showcases nine ways to drive loyalty and retention with these two critical groups.

### BLUE GOLDFISH - USING TECHNOLOGY, DATA, AND ANALYTICS TO DRIVE BOTH PROFITS AND PROPHETS

*Blue Goldfish* examines how to leverage technology, data, and analytics to do a "little something extra" to improve the experience for the customer. The book is based on a collection of over 300 case studies. It examines the three R's: Relationship, Responsiveness, and Readiness. *Blue Goldfish* uncovers eight different ways to turn insights into action.

### RED GOLDFISH - MOTIVATING SALES AND LOYALTY THROUGH SHARED PASSION AND PURPOSE

Purpose is changing the way we work and how customers choose business partners. It is driving loyalty, and it's on its way to becoming the ultimate differentiator in business. *Red Goldfish* shares cutting edge examples and reveals the eight ways businesses can embrace purpose that drives employee engagement, fuels the bottom line, and makes an impact on the lives of those it serves.

## PURPLE GOLDFISH SERVICE EDITION - 12 WAYS HOTELS, RESTAURANTS, AND AIRLINES WIN THE RIGHT CUSTOMERS

*Purple Goldfish Service Edition* is about differentiation via added value, and marketing to your existing customers via G.L.U.E. (**g**iving **l**ittle **u**nexpected **e**xtras). Packed with over 100 examples, the book focuses on the 12 ways to do the "little extras" to improve the customer experience for restaurants, hotels, and airlines. The end result is increased sales, happier customers, and positive word of mouth.

## PINK GOLDFISH - DEFY NORMAL, EXPLOIT IMPERFECTION, AND CAPTIVATE YOUR CUSTOMERS

Companies need to stand out in a crowded marketplace, but true differentiation is increasingly rare. Based on over 200 case studies, **Pink Goldfish** provides an unconventional seven-part framework for achieving competitive separation by embracing flaws instead of fixing them.

## PURPLE GOLDFISH FRANCHISE EDITION - THE ULTIMATE S.Y.S.T.E.M. FOR FRANCHISORS AND FRANCHISEES

Packed with over 100 best-practice examples, *Purple Goldfish Franchise Edition* focuses on the six keys to creating a successful franchise S.Y.S.T.E.M. and a dozen ways to create a signature customer experience.

## YELLOW GOLDFISH - NINE WAYS TO DRIVE HAPPINESS IN BUSINESS FOR GROWTH, PRODUCTIVITY, AND PROSPERITY

There should only be one success metric in business and that's happiness. A Yellow Goldfish is any time a business does a little extra to contribute to the happiness of its customers, employees, or society. Based on nearly 300 case studies, *Yellow Goldfish* provides a nine-part framework for happiness-driven growth, productivity, and prosperity in business.

## GRAY GOLDFISH - NAVIGATING THE GRAY AREAS TO SUCCESSFULLY LEAD EVERY GENERATION

How do you successfully lead the five generations in today's workforce? You need tools to navigate. Filled with over 100 case studies and the Generational Matrix, *Gray Goldfish* provides the definitive map for leaders to follow as they recruit, train, manage, and inspire across the generations.

## NOTES

Made in the USA
Monee, IL
01 July 2020